I Can Write

Anna Pomaska

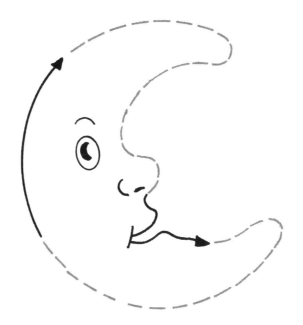

DOVER PUBLICATIONS, INC.
Mineola, New York

Note to Parents and Teachers

Young children will enjoy developing their writing skills in this appealing coloring book. Here are some helpful guidelines for its use: Ask children to say the letter at the top of the page (for example, "a"). Have them name each pictured object on that page (arrow, apple, ark, animals) and then trace over the dashed lines with a pencil or crayon, starting at the arrows. They will then trace each dashed line in the uppercase and lowercase letters at the top of the page, beginning at the arrows. Finally, they can practice writing the letters freehand at the bottom of each page in the ruled space after each example. You can provide tracing paper for additional practice.

Remember, young children's writing readiness will vary, so be patient with their efforts. When children have finished these activities, they can enjoy coloring the pages.

Copyright

Copyright © 2001 by Dover Publications, Inc.
All rights reserved under Pan American and International Copyright Conventions.

Bibliographical Note

I Can Write is a new work, first published by Dover Publications, Inc., in 2001.

DOVER *Pictorial Archive* SERIES

This book belongs to the Dover Pictorial Archive Series. You may use the designs and illustrations for graphics and crafts applications, free and without special permission, provided that you include no more than four in the same publication or project. (For permission for additional use, please write to Permissions Department, Dover Publications, Inc., 31 East 2nd Street, Mineola, N.Y. 11501.)

However, republication or reproduction of any illustration by any other graphic service, whether it be in a book or in any other design resource, is strictly prohibited.

International Standard Book Number: 0-486-41662-3

Manufactured in the United States of America
Dover Publications, Inc., 31 East 2nd Street, Mineola, N.Y. 11501

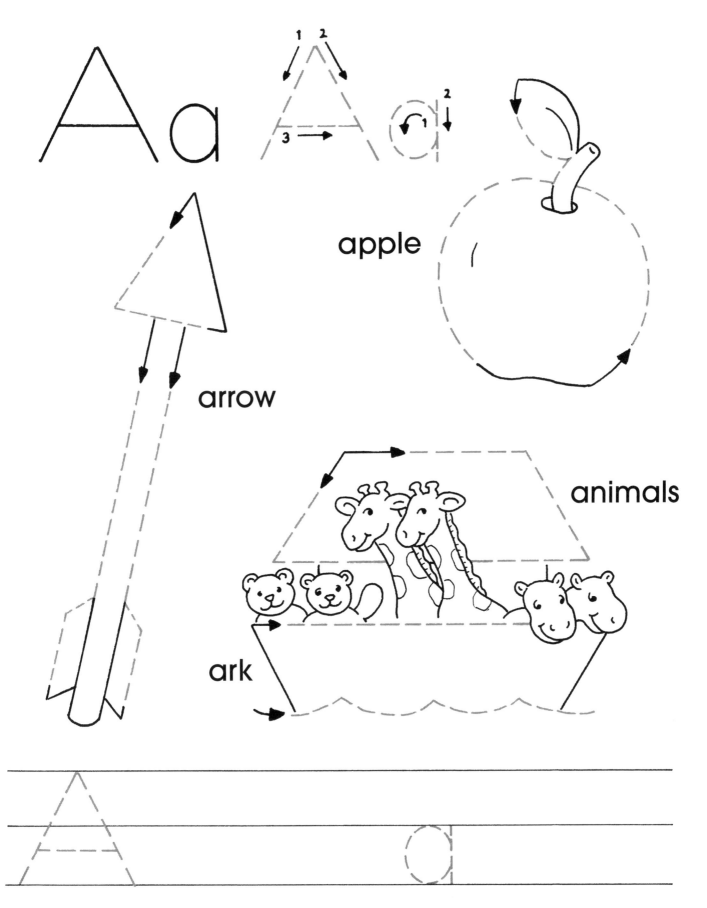

apple

arrow

animals

ark

B b

boat

balloon

bee

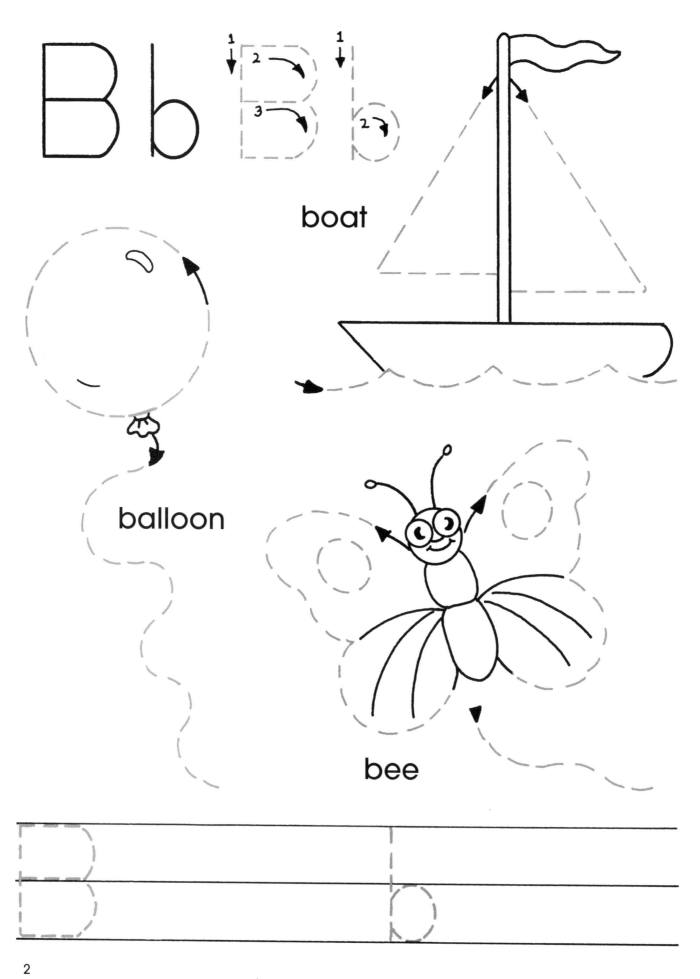

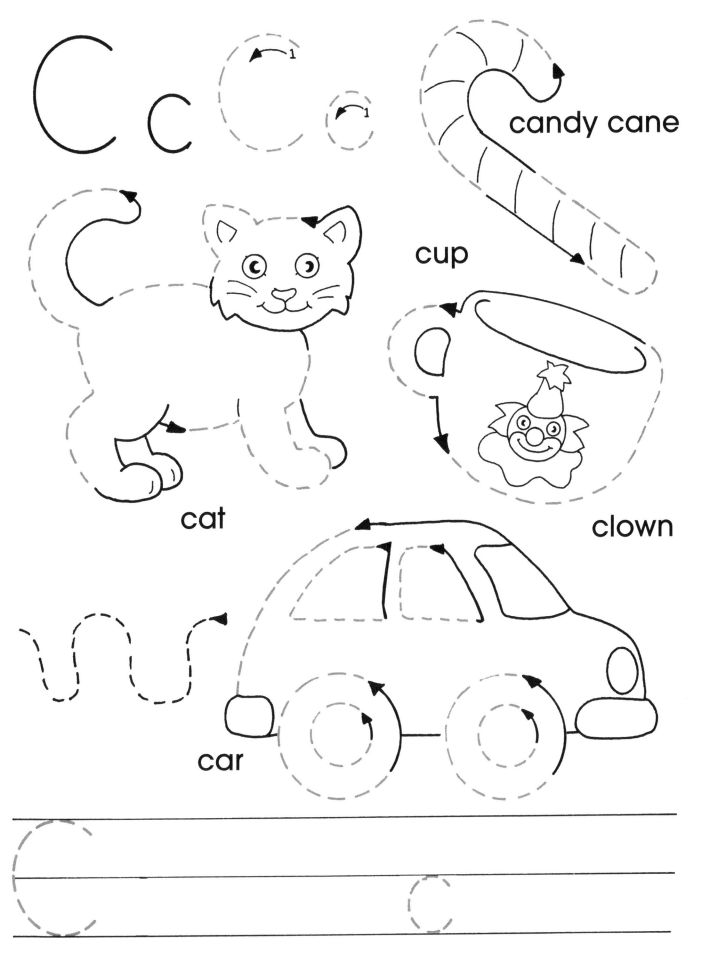

C c

candy cane

cup

cat

clown

car

Dd

duck

dinosaur

doll

dog

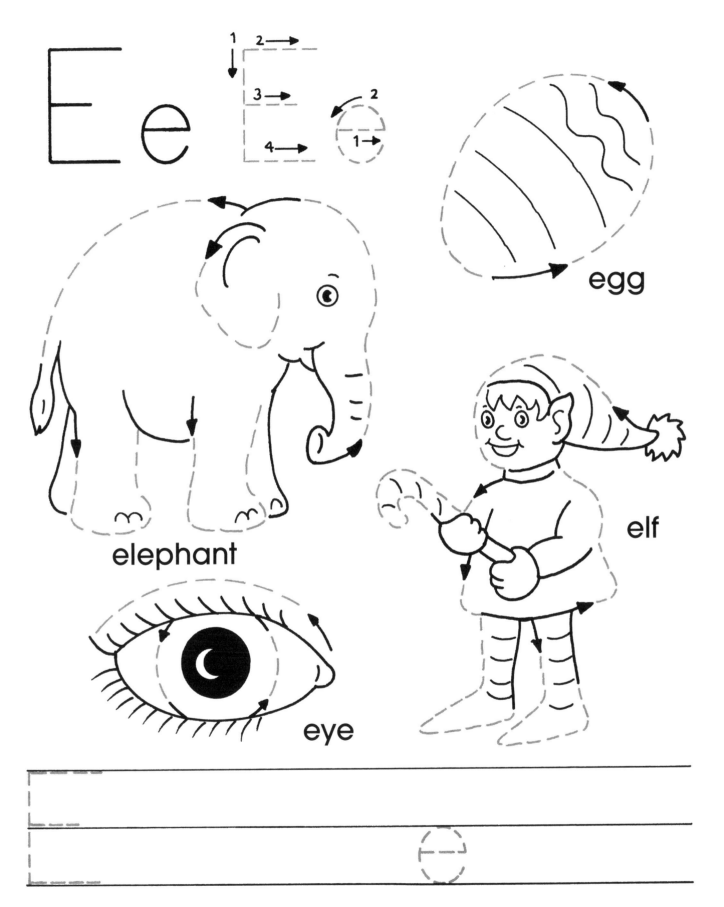

egg

elephant

elf

eye

5

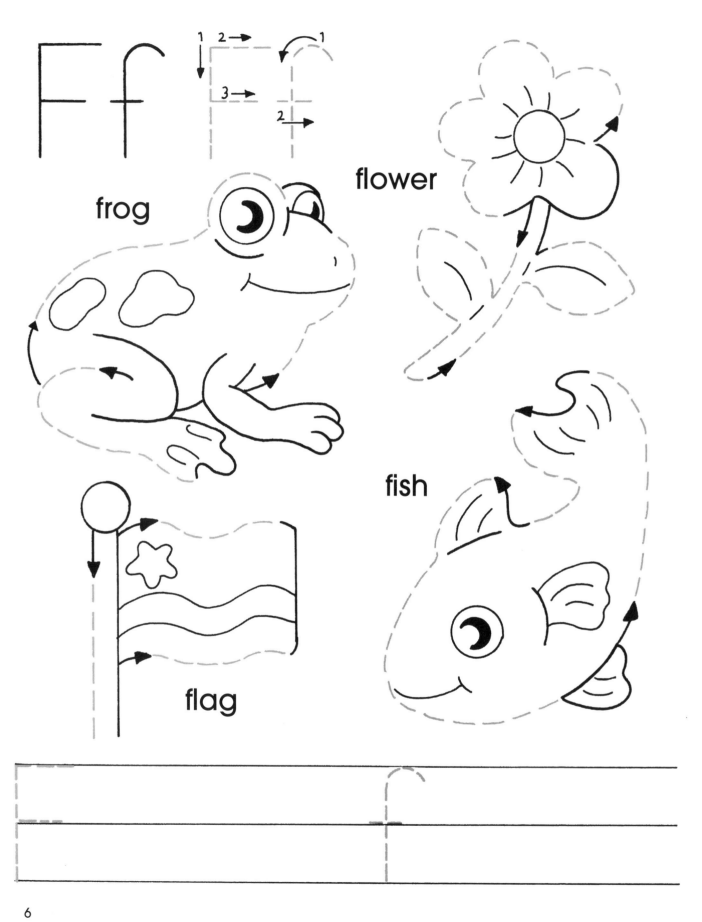

frog

flower

fish

flag

Gg

goose

ghost

goat

glasses

horn

hat

horse

house

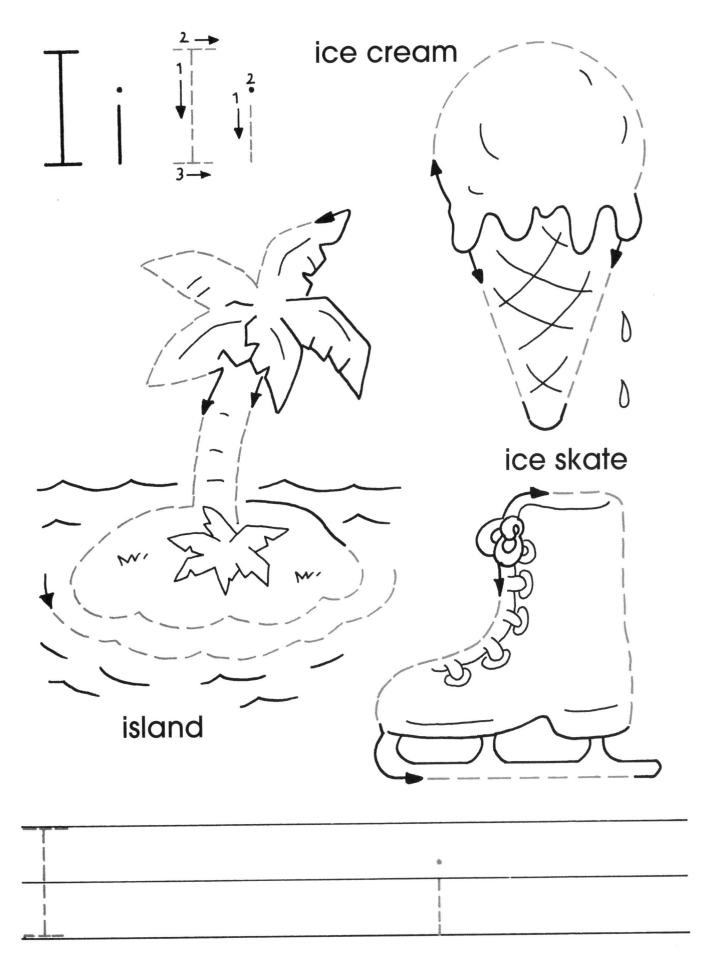

ice cream

ice skate

island

9

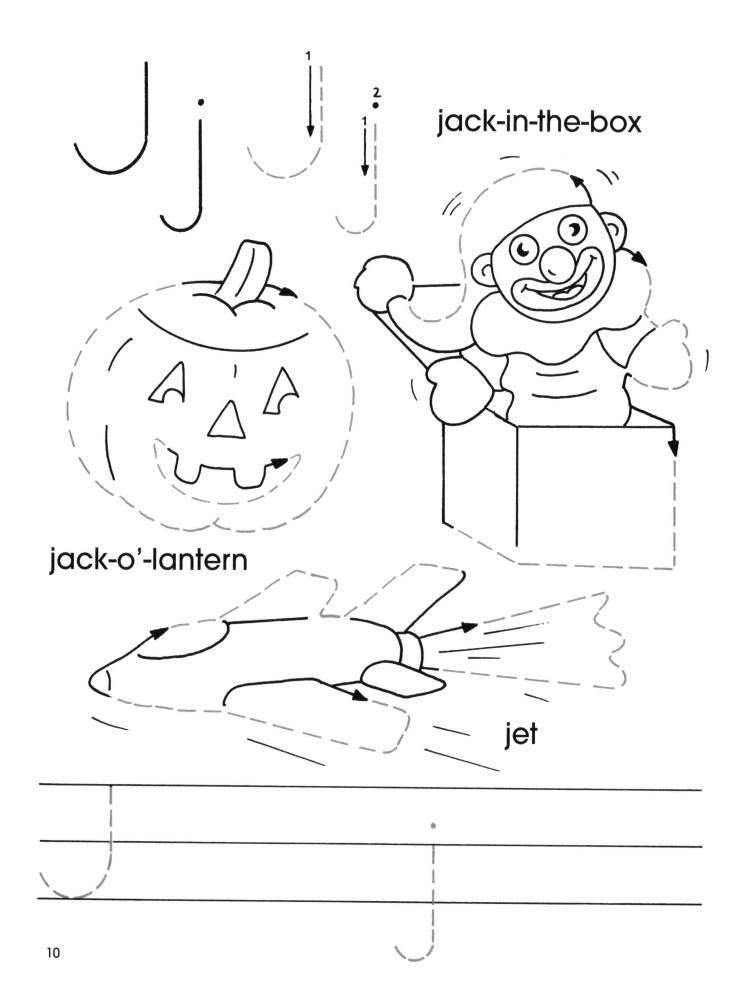

J j

jack-in-the-box

jack-o'-lantern

jet

key

kangaroo

kite

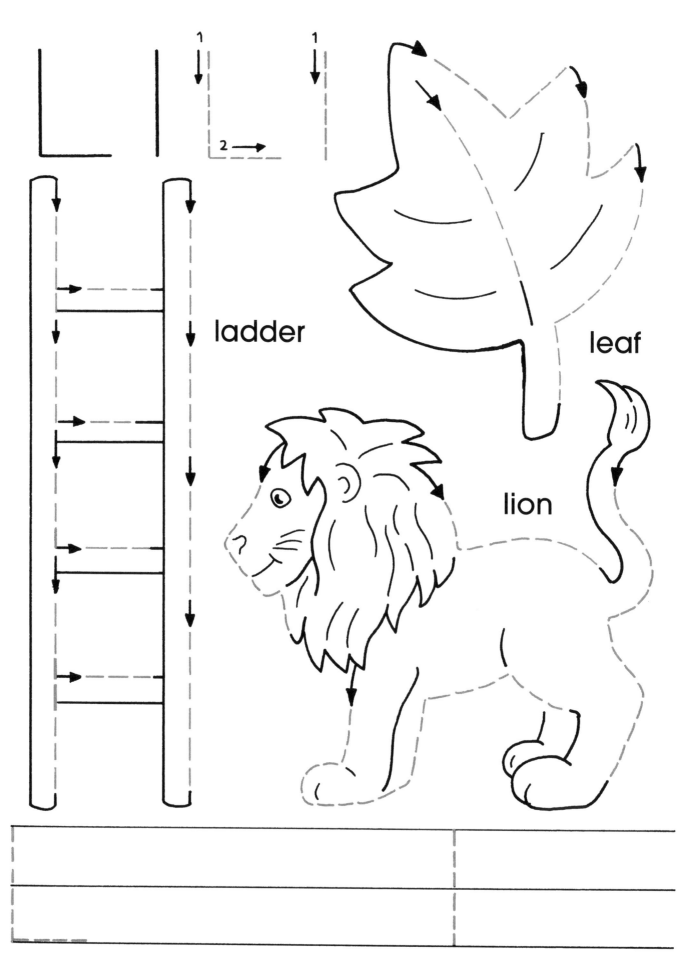

ladder

leaf

lion

Mm Mm

moon

mermaid

mouse

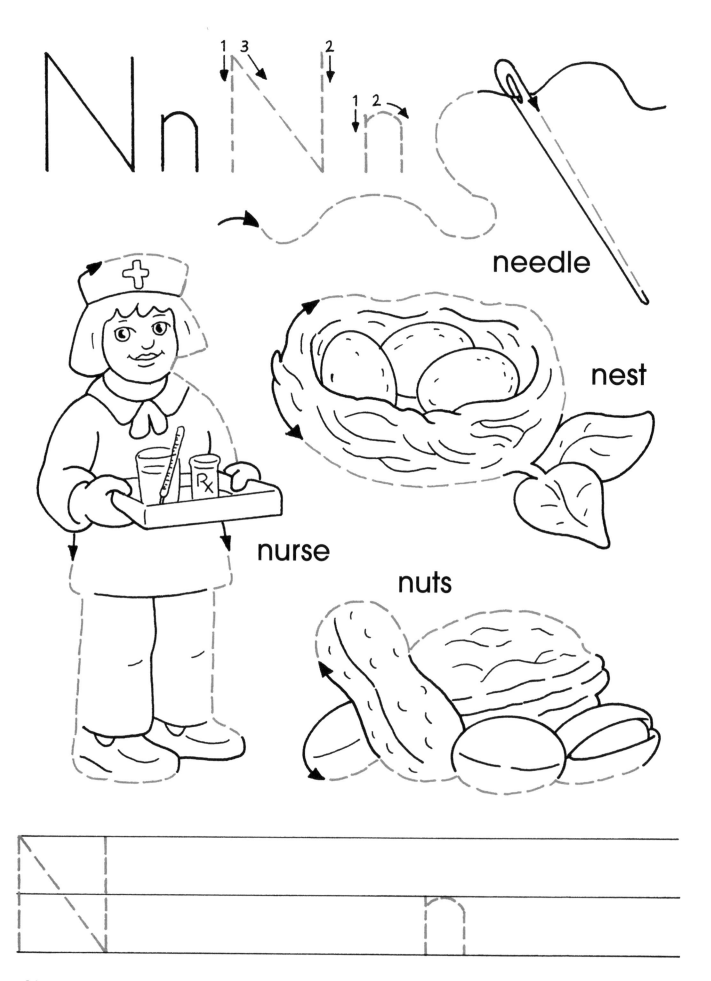

needle

nest

nurse

nuts

14

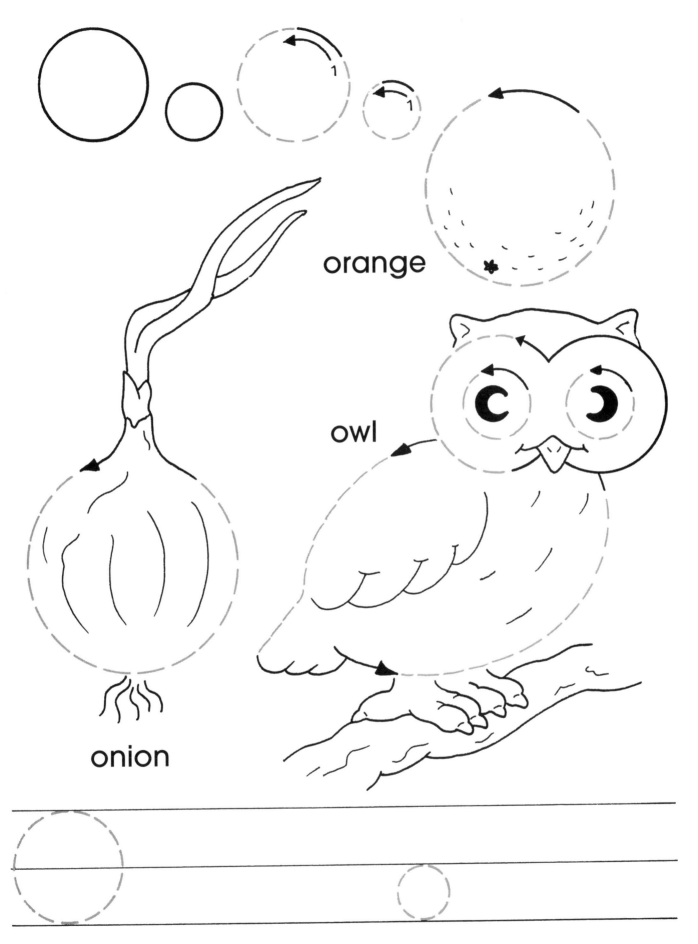

orange

owl

onion

15

pear

penguin

pie

pig

quilt

queen

17

rabbit

rocket

robot

snake

sun

squirrel

star

truck

tree

turtle

umbrella

unicorn

V v

I LOVE YOU!

valentine

vest

vulture

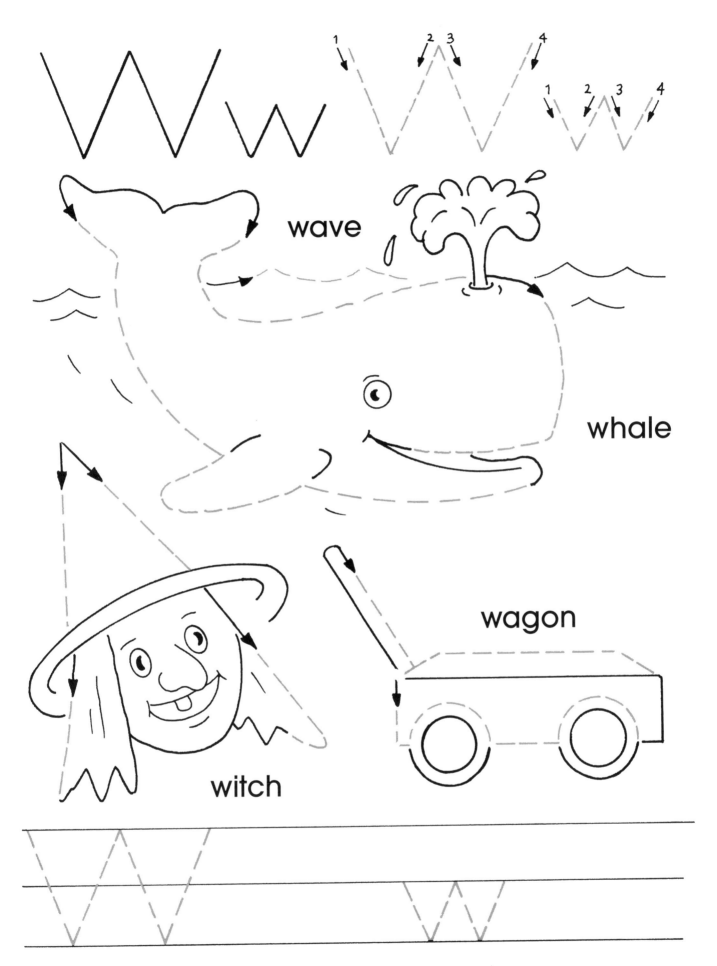

wave

whale

wagon

witch

xylophone

X ray

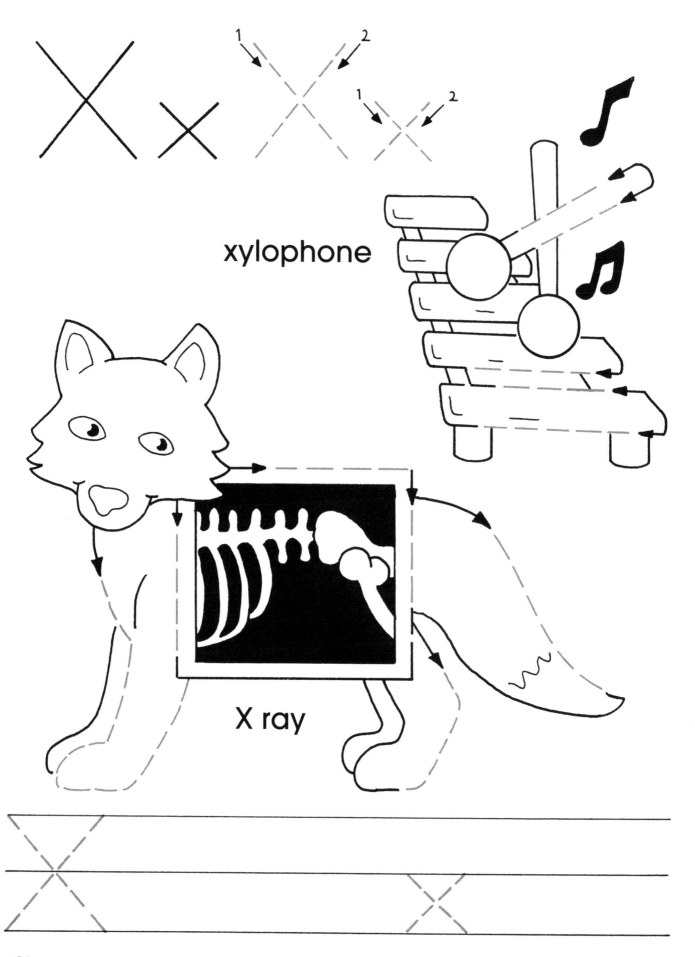

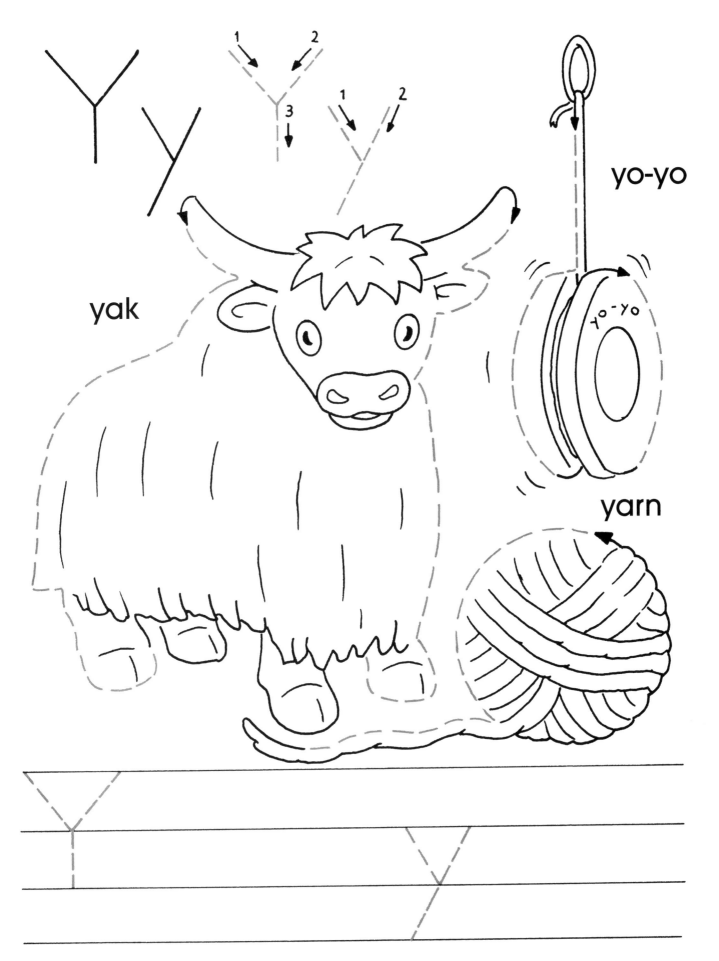

yak

yo-yo

yarn

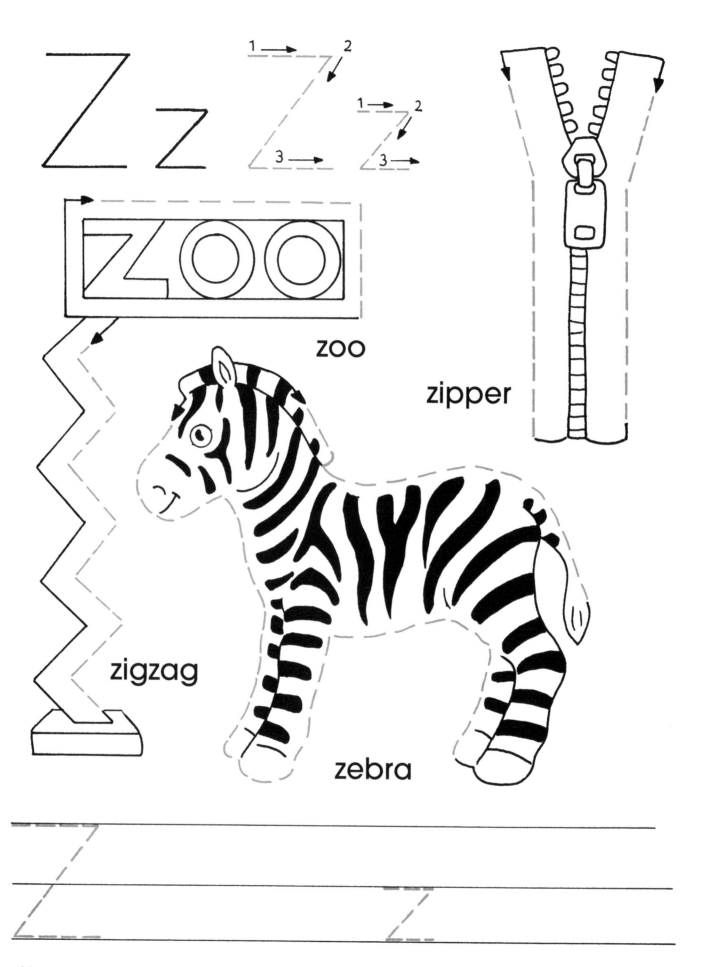

1 → 2

1 → 2

3 →

3 →

zoo

zipper

zigzag

zebra

Directions: Trace each letter at the top of the page. Then find the picture that starts with that letter (C—Cat). Write the letter on the lines next to the picture. (The first one has been done for you.) When you are finished, you can enjoy coloring in the pictures.

27